Lettering

Make Your Own Cards, Signs, Gifts and More

Written by
Amanda Lewis

Illustrated by
Esperança Melo

Kids Can Press Ltd.

For Tim, through **thick** and thin

Acknowledgments

My sincere thanks go to Esperança Melo for her wonderful illustrations and fresh ideas; to Heather Mallett for her astute criticisms of my Gothic ductus; to Nancy Culmone for her pencil crayon ideas; and to the great-granddaddy of contemporary calligraphy, Edward Johnston, for his methodology and his double pencil technique. I have also greatly appreciated the support of the Ontario Arts Council. This book would never have seen the light of day had it not been for the stalwart Liz MacLeod, an editor who always knows the right thing to say, and the support of the great Kids Can team.

Kids Can Press Ltd. acknowledges with appreciation the assistance of the Canada Council and the Ontario Arts Council in the production of this book.

Canadian Cataloguing in Publication Data

Lewis, Amanda
Lettering : make your own cards, signs, gifts and more

(Kids Can crafts)
ISBN 1-55074-312-0 (bound)   ISBN 1-55074-232-9 (pbk.)

1. Lettering — Juvenile literature. 2. Handicraft — Juvenile literature.
I. Melo, Esperança. II. Title. III. Series

TT360.L48 1995   j745.6'1   C95-931908-5

First U.S. edition 1997

Published by:
Kids Can Press Ltd.
29 Birch Avenue
Toronto, Ontario, Canada
M4V 1E2

Published in the U.S. by:
Kids Can Press Ltd.
85 River Rock Drive, Suite 202
Buffalo, NY 14207

Edited by Elizabeth MacLeod
Designed by Karen Powers
Printed in Hong Kong

97 0987654321

Contents

CHAPTER 1 Big messages
Double pencils 4
Welcome home banner (Variation: Cloth banner) 6
Room sign 8

CHAPTER 2 Greetings
Learn Gothic calligraphy 10
Place cards 14
Invitations (Variation: Holiday cards) 16
Award scroll 18

CHAPTER 3 Attention grabbers
Project cover 20
Rock poster (Variation: Other posters) 24

CHAPTER 4 Computer-ease
Letterhead 26
Newsletter 28

CHAPTER 5 Playful letters
Flyer 30
Calligram calendar 33

CHAPTER 6 Beautiful letters
Versal letters 36
Gift tag (Variation: Labels) 38

CHAPTER 7 Book works
Book mark 40
Book plate (Variation: Illuminated story or poem) 42

CHAPTER 8 3-D letters
Congratulations letter tower 44
Earrings (Variation: Pins and necklaces) 46

Keep lettering 48

CHAPTER ONE

Big messages

These projects use large letters that are easy to see from a distance. Large letters need to have wide letter lines called strokes. An easy way to make wide lines is to use two pencils attached together, or "double pencils."

YOU WILL NEED

two sharp pencils, the same kind and length

two elastic bands

masking tape (optional)

scrap paper

two or more coloured pencils

DOUBLE PENCILS

1 Attach your two pencils tightly together with the elastic bands — one at the top and one at the bottom of the pencils. Hold them as if they were one thick pencil. If they slip, use masking tape to hold them firmly in place.

2 Using your double pencils, make zigzags, spirals and other patterns on your scrap paper. If one line is lighter than the other, your pencils might not be even or you may be pressing too hard on one side. Adjust the pencils until they feel as if they are both touching the page in the same way at the same time.

3 Changing the way you hold the pencils will affect how your lines look. Try holding them in different ways:

Straight to the page

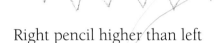

Right pencil higher than left

4 Using your coloured pencils, fill in the space between the lines. Try thinking of your pattern as a ribbon, and use one colour for one side and a different colour for the other side. You'll get a 3-D effect if you colour the space lightly and more darkly, as shown.

For another effect, use two different coloured pencils for your double pencils and fill in the spaces with a third colour.

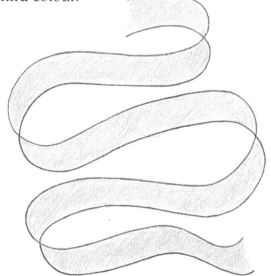

Welcome home banner

Make this long paper banner to show friends how much you've missed them.

YOU WILL NEED

five sheets of paper 21.5 cm x 28 cm
(8½ inches x 11 inches)

double pencils (see page 4)

coloured markers

pencil, eraser, ruler, scissors,
sticky tape

1 Tape your paper together end to end so you have one piece 140 cm (55 inches) long. Put the tape on the back side of the paper. Or use five sheets of computer paper that are already attached and tape the joins.

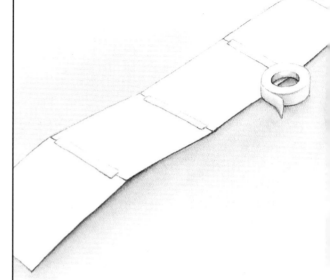

2 Draw guidelines to keep your writing straight by making light pencil marks 5.5 cm and 14 cm (2⅛ inches and 5½ inches) from the top of the banner. Do this at several places, then lightly connect these marks.

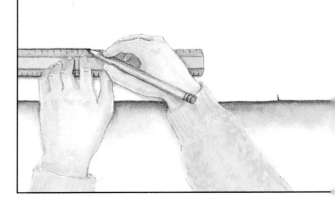

3 Starting about 10 cm (4 inches) from the left side of your paper, use your double pencils to print WELCOME HOME in capital letters between the two guidelines.

4 Fill in the letters with your markers. You can also go over the pencil lines with marker.

5 Carefully erase your guidelines. Cut off any extra paper, leaving the same-size margin at either end of your message.

WELCOME HOME

VARIATION: CLOTH BANNER

You can make a really special and permanent banner on cloth. Felt is a good material to use. Follow the instructions for the welcome home banner but use chalk instead of pencil to make your guidelines. Go over your double pencil lines with a dark marker or fabric paint. If you use puffy paint your letters will really stand out. Fill in the lines using a different colour of marker or fabric paint.

Room sign

Use double pencils to make a sign for your door. In this project you'll write small letters as well as capital letters.

1 Tape the construction paper together end to end. Tape on the back side of the paper only. Mark off guidelines as you did with the banner (page 6) at 2 cm, 5 cm, 10 cm, 12 cm, and 17 cm (³/₄ inch, 2 inches, 4 inches, 4³/₄ inches, 6³/₄ inches) from the top of the paper.

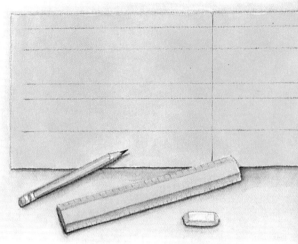

2 Using your double pencils, print your name followed by 's in the top three guidelines.

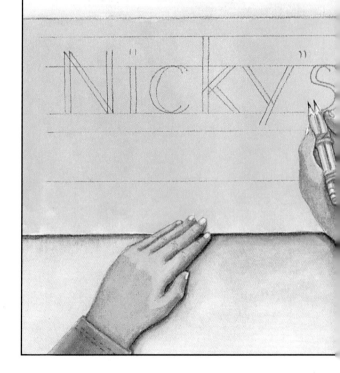

3 Print the word "room" in the bottom two guidelines, using small letters as shown.

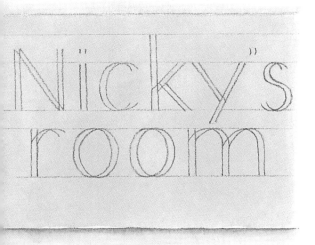

4 Use markers or coloured pencils to outline the letters and fill them in. Carefully erase your guidelines. To make a border for your sign, see GOOD IDEA on this page. Cut off any extra paper.

GOOD IDEA

GOOD IDEA: BORDERS

The shapes you make when you write can be used to make borders on cards, invitations, signs, etc. Start with a simple letter shape and repeat it. Try to think of an image to go with the pattern, such as

a bouncing ball

cartwheels

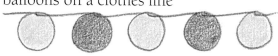

balloons on a clothes line

a flowing river

If you are putting a border on something you've already written, the "shape" of the writing can determine the shape of your border.

CHAPTER TWO

Greetings

If you have something really special or important you want to say, try writing it in Gothic lettering. Small Gothic letters use only straight lines — only the capitals have curves or circles — and the lines are very close to one another.

YOU WILL NEED

graph paper with squares 0.5 cm x 0.5 cm (¼ inch x ¼ inch)

double pencils (see page 4)

a broad-size calligraphy pen or marker with a nib or edge about 2.5 mm (⅛ inch) wide (see GOOD IDEA on this page)

pencil, eraser, ruler

LEARN GOTHIC CALLIGRAPHY

GOOD IDEA: CALLIGRAPHY PENS AND MARKERS

For the calligraphy projects on pages 14 to 19, you'll need calligraphy pens or markers. These pens and markers are different from ordinary pens and markers because they have a "chisel" edge. That means they don't come to a point at the end, but instead have a wide, flat end.

Chisel-edged pens

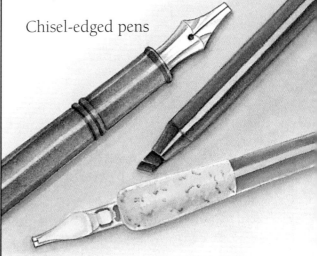

You'll find many kinds of calligraphy pens and markers in stationery and art supply stores. Markers are easier to use because they are always ready — they don't need to be filled. However, they will eventually run out of ink and get bent out of shape. If you want to do a lot of calligraphy, get a calligraphy pen or pen set. A pen set includes different widths of pen endings, called nibs. If you are left-handed, you will need to find a left-handed calligraphy pen or pen set. They are harder to get but look for ones by Osmiroid or Platignum. (You can use the same markers whether you're right- or left-handed.)

1 To practise your lettering, you'll need to make some guidelines on your graph paper. With your pencil and ruler, make lines as shown:

ascender line: tall letters like h reach to here

x-height line: it's the same height as the letter x

You'll write the body of your letters in the middle space.

baseline: all your letters sit on this line

descender line: long letters likely reach to here

2 It's a little easier to learn calligraphy if you practise with double pencils first. Hold them so the right-side pencil is touching the top guideline and the left-side pencil is below it at a 45° angle. Pull straight down until your left pencil touches the baseline. Your right pencil should still be higher. This is called a 45° pen angle. Practise drawing lines straight down from the x-height to the baseline. The graph paper will help you keep your lines straight.

3 Now, holding your double pencils the same way, draw horizontal lines. They should be the same width as your vertical lines.

4 Switch to your calligraphy pen or marker. Draw guidelines one square, two squares and one square apart. Make vertical and horizontal lines at a 45° pen angle as you did with your double pencils.

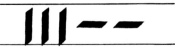

5 Next, try putting thick diagonal tops and bottoms on the strokes. A diamond dot over the top makes an i.

6 Gothic letters are made by putting together these vertical, horizontal and diagonal strokes. The Gothic alphabet is shown here. The letters are not in order, but are in groups of letters that are all made the same way. The numbers show the order of the strokes, and the arrows show the direction in which to move your pen. Make sure the space inside the letter (called a counter) looks like a long rectangle, not a square.

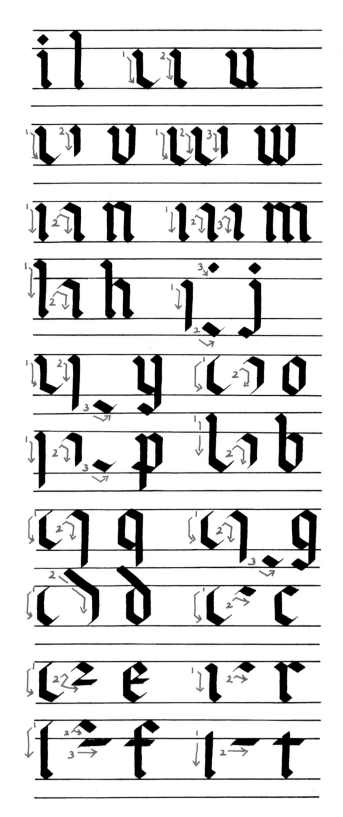

7 When you write capital letters you'll have to make some round strokes — just keep holding your pen at the 45° angle. Make your capital letters two-and-a-half squares high on your graph paper.

a b c d

e f g h i

j k l m

n o p q r

s t u v

w x y z

A B C

D E F

G H I J

K L M

N O P

Q R S

T U V

W X Y Z

Place cards

Use Gothic lettering to make truly elegant place cards for your next special dinner.

YOU WILL NEED

lined index cards 10.2 cm x 15.5 cm
(4$\frac{1}{8}$ inches x 6$\frac{1}{8}$ inches)

a broad calligraphy pen or marker

pencil, eraser, ruler

1 You can write directly on the lined side of the index cards or on the blank back — with a good light you should be able to see through to the lines on the other side. Count up three lines from the bottom of your card. This will be your baseline. You can darken it with a pencil and a ruler if you like. Use the next line up as your x-height line. Rule an ascender line 0.3 cm ($\frac{1}{8}$ inch) above it and a descender line 0.3 cm ($\frac{1}{8}$ inch) below the baseline.

2 Beginning about 2.5 cm (1 inch) from the left side, write a guest's name in Gothic letters. Begin with a capital and keep your letters close together — there should be no more than the width of a stroke between each letter. You may have room for only the first name.

Timothy

3 Repeat for all your guests. Let your ink dry for at least five minutes, erase any lines you drew, then fold the card in half lengthwise. Decorate the edges and the back with vines or decorations if you like (see page 41).

GOOD IDEA: CHANGING PEN SIZES
You can change the size of your writing by using a smaller pen. But you'll have to change your guideline size, too. To find the best size, turn your pen so the entire flat edge is straight on a vertical line on your graph paper. Draw a short horizontal stroke. It should be the thickest line your pen can make.

That's called your "pen-width."

Line up four pen-widths, one right on top of the other. Measure how tall they are. That will be your x-height (see page 11). In Gothic lettering the x-height is four pen-widths, the ascenders and decenders are each two pen-widths, and your capitals are about six pen-widths. These proportions work for any size of Gothic lettering.

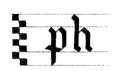 

Invitations

Show your friends you care by sending out special invitations for your next party.

YOU WILL NEED

three or four pieces of white paper 21.5 cm x 28 cm ($8\frac{1}{2}$ inches x 11 inches)

calligraphy pens or markers in different sizes

access to a photocopier

correction fluid such as White Out or Liquid Paper

pencil, ruler, eraser, scissors, glue stick, scrap paper

1 Cut a piece of paper to measure 17 cm x 28 cm ($6\frac{3}{4}$ inches x 11 inches). This will fit into a standard 9 cm x 16.5 cm ($3\frac{1}{2}$ inches x $6\frac{1}{2}$ inches) envelope. You'll use this page for your original invitation.

Fold it in half widthwise. Then fold it in half again, the other way.

2 On the scrap paper, make a list of what your invitation will say: the time, place, day of the party, and any special information. (Is it a surprise party? A costume party? A sleepover?)

3 On a piece of white paper, make some guidelines for your largest-size nib (see page 15). With your calligraphy pen, write out the words "You're Invited," "Surprise!" or "Party" — whatever you want to say on the front of your invitation.

4 Cut out your words and place them on the front of the folded paper. Try them in different places. Glue them on where you think they look best.

5 On your white paper rule some guidelines for a smaller pen size. (See page 15 for changing pen sizes.) Write out all the invitation information line by line. Don't make any line longer than 14 cm (5½ inches). If you make a mistake, begin that line again. When you have all the information written correctly, carefully erase your guidelines and cut out each line.

6 Open your invitation to the inside and place each line you cut out where you want it. When you like the way the lines look together, glue them in place.

7 If you want to add a border to the page, turn to page 9.

8 Unfold your page and photocopy it. You may want to photocopy your invitations onto coloured paper. If the copy has lines on it from the edges of your cut-out lines, carefully white them out on the copy, then copy the copy.

9 Fold and deliver your invitations.

VARIATION: HOLIDAY CARDS
You can make cards to celebrate a holiday by following the instructions for making invitations. Stickers or designs made with coloured markers can be added to each card.

Award scroll

A scroll is a great way to present someone with an award. Your scroll could be a serious or a funny way to show your appreciation to someone, or to celebrate something special.

YOU WILL NEED

graph paper or scrap paper for practice

two sizes of calligraphy pen or marker

a piece of legal size paper 21.5 cm x 35.5 cm (8½ inches x 14 inches) — try to find coloured paper

ordinary pen or marker

lined paper

a piece of ribbon, 50 cm x 1 cm (20 inches x ³/₈ inch)

pencil, eraser, ruler, scissors or X-acto knife, sticky tape

1 Decide what your scroll will say. You'll need a title, such as "Award of Excellence," "Certificate of Friendship" or "Best Dog." Then say something about whoever is receiving the award and why he or she is special.

2 Practise writing the title in Gothic lettering (see page 12) on your scrap paper with a medium-size calligraphy pen. Use an x-height of four pen-widths, and descenders and ascenders of two pen-widths.

Best Dog

3 Lightly rule guidelines for your medium-size pen on your long piece of paper, beginning about 5 cm (2 inches) from the top. Rule a guideline down the centre of the page as well.

4 Cut out your practice title. Fold it in the middle widthwise and place the fold on the centre line. Mark the left edge of the writing lightly with your pencil. This will help you place your title in the centre of the page.

5 Starting at the point you just marked, write your title on your long sheet of paper.

6 Using a larger-size calligraphy pen and Gothic lettering, practise writing the name of the person who is receiving the scroll on your scrap paper. (Remember to use larger guidelines.) Cut out the name and fold it widthwise in the middle.

7 Draw guidelines for the name on the long piece of paper, beginning about 10 cm (4 inches) from the top of the page. Place the name on the guidelines, matching the fold and the centre line. Mark where the name begins and then write it out on the guidelines.

8 Tape your lined paper to your writing surface. Put your scroll on top, matching up a guideline on your scroll with one of the lines on the paper. With an ordinary pen or marker and your regular printing style, print out any other information about the scroll, using the lined paper underneath for guidelines. Include the date and your signature, and decorate the scroll.

9 Mark two small horizontal lines 1 cm (³/₈ inch) long on the centre line at 3 cm (1¹/₄ inches) and at 5 cm (2 inches) from the bottom of the page. Cut along these lines carefully with scissors or an X-acto knife (ask an adult to help you). Erase all guidelines.

10 Thread the ribbon from the back through the slit farthest from the bottom, then through the other slit to the back. When you roll up your scroll you can use this ribbon to tie it.

CHAPTER THREE

Attention grabbers

What's design? It's the choices you make about how you want things to look. This section has projects with designs that will make your ideas more eye-catching.

YOU WILL NEED

coloured construction paper

coloured pencils and/or markers

one piece of light-coloured
bristol board 43.2 cm x 28 cm
(17 inches x 11 inches)

illustrations from magazines (optional)

pencil, eraser, ruler, scissors,
glue stick, scrap paper

PROJECT COVER

Making a cover for a school project will protect your work and make the project look special.

1 On scrap paper, write out the title of your project and the subtitle, if you have one. Collect any pictures you want to include on the cover.

2 On your scrap paper write as many descriptive words about your project as possible. For example, if your project is about electricity, you might write: energy, jolt, jagged, jarring, exciting, bright and sparks.

3 Choose construction paper and some coloured pencils that seem to match those words. For example, for the word "electricity" you might use silver, yellow and white on black paper, or maybe orange and red on blue paper.

4 You need to experiment with your word to find a "look" you like. Try these variations in lettering styles:

- Print your word, using the side of your pencil so that you get wide lines. Make your letters at least 2.5 cm (1 inch) high.

ELEC

- Print the word again, changing the kind of lines you use to make the letters. Try writing ELECTRICITY with jagged, spiky lines. Other words might use fat, round lines or dotted lines.

ELEC

- Try more variations, using different colours, styles and placements. Keep checking your list of descriptive words for ideas. See pages 5 and 25 for more ideas on using coloured pencils.

Elect

5 Pick your favourite variation and cut it out.

6 Your bristol board will wrap around your project. Fold it in half widthwise. Experiment to decide where to place your title on the half that forms the front cover. See page 25 for ideas about placement on the page. Glue your title in place.

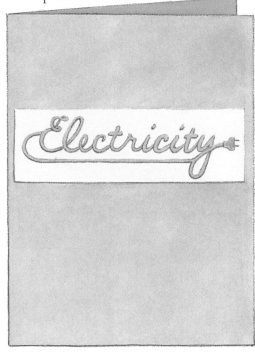

7 If you have a subtitle, print it on your construction paper in letters about 1.5 cm (½ inch) high, using the same combinations of style and colour as you did with your title.

8 Cut out your subtitle and place it below your title. Glue it in place.

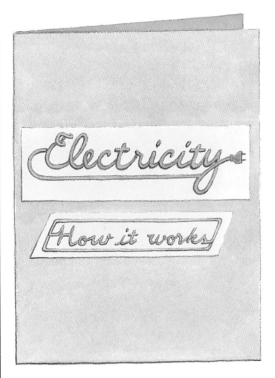

9 Draw guidelines 4 cm (1½ inches), 5 cm (2 inches), 7 cm (2¾ inches) and 7.5 cm (3 inches) from the bottom of the bristol board. Using a pencil, print your name between the lower pair of guidelines leaving lots of space around each letter.

10 Print "by" in the centre of the top set of guidelines. Go over all the letters with marker.

11 Let your marker lines dry thoroughly before rubbing out your pencil lines. Glue any pictures you want to include on the cover. Check page 9 for ideas on borders and decorations. Place or staple your project inside the cover.

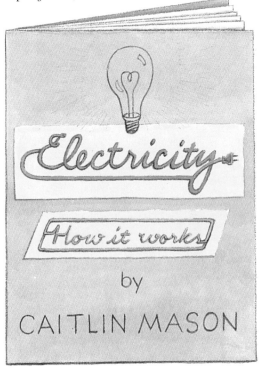

GOOD IDEA: PLACEMENT ON THE PAGE

Some places on a page naturally attract your eye's attention. Here are some strong placements on a page:

The optical centre is above the true centre of the page. If you want something to look as if it's in the centre of the page, you have to place it on the optical centre.

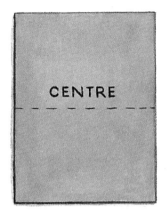

Diagonal placement is good for longer words.

Subtitles or smaller headings can be placed in different positions from the main heading for contrast.

GOOD IDEA: WRITING ON A CURVE

If you want to write neatly on a curve, use a compass to make your guidelines. Put your compass point in the centre of the area you want to write in, stretch the arm until it makes the curve size you want, then draw your first line. Measure and mark out guidelines.

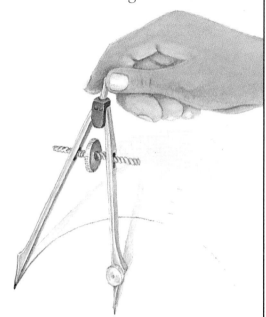

Keep the compass point fixed in the centre and stretch out the arm to draw each line. When you write on curved guidelines, you need to keep turning your page so you are always writing straight up and down on the lines.

Rock poster

Are any of your friends in a band or a musical group? You can use design principles to make a poster for their next performance. Or you can create a poster for your favourite rock group.

1 On scrap paper, list the information to go on your poster in order of importance. For example, you'll want to include the name of the group, the time, date and place the group is playing, and any admission fee that's being charged. You might want to describe the kind of music they play. Is it rocking, kicking and heavy, or is it sweet, gentle and light?

2 Choose the most important information and experiment with different lettering styles and colours to get a combination that is right for your group. Try cutting letters out of construction paper or even out of magazines. Keep the letters big and bold. Follow the lettering variations suggested on page 21.

3 See page 23 to find the best placement for your lettering. If you want to have illustrations on the poster (such as pictures of guitars or screaming fans), put them on first and then try gluing letters over the pictures.

4 Follow steps 7 to 10 on pages 21–22 for ideas about subheadings, etc. For suggestions on design principles, see GOOD IDEA on this page.

VARIATION: OTHER POSTERS

You can make many other kinds of posters to advertise a play, a garage sale or a special event. Use materials listed for the rock poster (page 24), suggestions for design principles (right), and ideas for placement on the page (page 23) and for lettering variations (page 21) to create your own designs.

GOOD IDEA: DESIGN PRINCIPLES

- Don't use more than two or three styles or sizes of lettering on one page.
- Leave lots of space around your letters and around the edges of the page.
- The optical centre is above the true centre of the page.
- Cool colours, such as blue, green or purple, "retreat." They seem to go back into the page.

- Hot colours, such as red, orange or yellow, "advance." They seem to jump off the page.

- Heavy letters have wide strokes compared with their height, while light letters have thin strokes compared with their height.

Computer-ease

You can design many different projects with the variety of lettering styles on your computer. Computers can be very useful for designing a page that you want to look the same every time.

LETTERHEAD

Letterhead is stationery that has your name and address on it. With this project you can design your own letterhead to use every time you write a letter.

1 Open your computer to a word-processing program. Create a new file called "Letterhead."

2 Choose what font or fonts you want your letterhead to be in. Here are some examples of fonts found in many word-processing programs.

Palatino	Classic and elegant
Helvetica	Clean and no-nonsense
STENCIL	Technical and bold
Parisian	Stylish and fun
Zapf Chancery	Looks like handwriting
Times	Intelligent-looking
Tekton	Friendly and simple

3 Type your name in the font you've picked. With some computers, the letters on the screen look different from the final printed version. You may have to use your imagination a bit.

4 You need to enlarge your name to make it stand out. Type letters are measured in a special measurement size called a "point." There are 72 points in 2.5 cm (1 inch). Your computer will have a number of standard point sizes for your fonts. Smaller point sizes mean smaller letters. Letters in 18- or 24-point type would be good for your name.

Alison Good

18 point

Alison Good

24 point

5 Formatting on a computer means the way you treat your letters. Formats include underlining, italic, outlining and bold. Format your name to print in bold.

Alison Good

6 Use your computer to centre your name near the top of your page.

Alison Good

7 In 14-point type and regular, not bold, lettering, type your address below your name. Keep all the information centred under your name.

Alison Good

93 West Musgrave Street
Cedar Springs, Iowa
52240-3211

8 When you've typed in all the information, print it out to see what it looks like. You can add a margin around the page, using symbols on your computer. Or find the bottom of your page and put your initials — very large — in the centre. Experiment and make changes until you've got your page the way you want it.

9 Save your new letterhead file. It will be there whenever you want to type a letter. If you type a letter that you want to save, you have to save it as something else (for example, "Letter to ..."). Otherwise, you will end up changing your letterhead file permanently.

Newsletter

If you put out a newsletter, you can design it using the same method you used to make your letterhead and using the design principles that are on page 25.

1 Make a list of the information you want to appear in each newsletter. For example, you'll want a title, subtitle, and headings such as Jokes, Ads, General News and Sports.

2 Create a new file called Newsletter.

3 Decide on the font, point size and format you want for your newsletter title. Experiment with formats like bold, outline, and shadow.

BROOKE VALLEY NEWS

BROOKE VALLEY NEWS

BROOKE VALLEY NEWS

4 When you have a title you like, centre it on the page.

5 If you have a subtitle, it should be in a plainer and smaller type than your title. It could also be in another font. Experiment with your subtitle, then centre it under your title.

BROOKE VALLEY NEWS

A Monthly Newsletter of Valley Events

6 Pick a font, point size and format for your headings in the newsletter. They can be centred on your page or put into columns as needed.

7 Once you've typed in all your headings, print them out to see how they look. Save your newsletter file when you've finished.

8 When you are ready to create a newsletter, open your newsletter file, type in it, and then save it as something else (for example, April News). This way you'll always have your original newsletter file to use. You can move or delete any of your headings as you need.

BROOKE VALLEY NEWS

A Monthly Newsletter of Valley Events

News in the valley

Ads

Birthdays

Sports

Jokes

Coming events

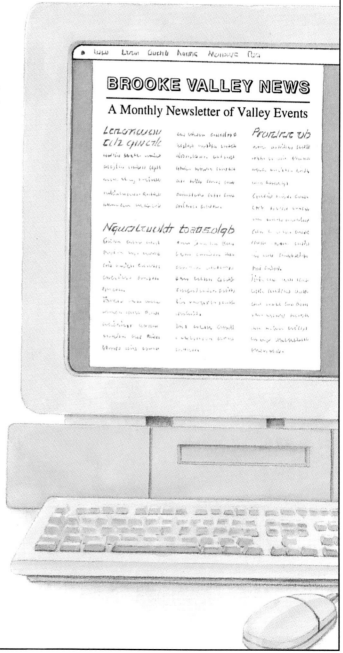

CHAPTER FIVE

Playful letters

Long ago, letters were pictures. It's still fun to treat them as lively pictures that can be read. In this section you'll make exciting letters that have a life of their own.

YOU WILL NEED

two pieces of white paper 21.5 cm x 28 cm (8½ inches x 11 inches)

thin black marker

one piece of lined paper

thin calligraphy marker (optional)

markers or coloured pencils

access to a photocopier

pencil, eraser, ruler, scissors, sticky tape, glue stick, scrap paper

FLYER

An advertisement tells people about things they might want to buy, see or do. One way of doing this is to make a flyer to hand out or put into mailboxes.

1 Decide what information you want on your flyer. Write it down on your scrap paper in order of importance: what you want to sell or do, a description of it, the price, your name, phone number, etc.

2 Make your heading as simple as possible. For example, Bike or Baby-sitting Service. Can you make those words look like what they represent or include drawings that relate to them? Think about what you want your letters to say, and what kinds of lines or shapes suggest that idea.

For example, letters can look scared

look cheerful

Putting letters on a slant and drawing "speed lines" behind them makes you think of a bike whizzing along.

These letters are pudgy, bouncy and round, like a baby. The diapers and pin relate to the idea, too.

3 When you decide on a style you like, write your heading in pencil on a blank paper, making sure your letters are at least 2 to 4 cm ($^3/_4$ to $1^1/_2$ inches) tall.

4 Trace over your lines with the marker to make them more visible.

5 Cut out your heading and glue it on a fresh piece of paper about 5 cm (2 inches) from the top of the page.

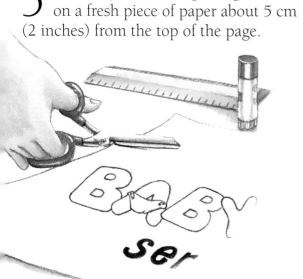

6 Tape a piece of lined paper to your writing surface, then lightly tape your paper with the heading onto it. Write out the next-most-important information in capital letters under your heading, using the lines on your lined paper to guide you. Write in pencil first to make sure the words will fit, then go over them with your marker.

If the letters look too light or thin compared with your heading, thicken them by tracing over each stroke several times. Or use a thin calligraphy marker to print them (see page 10).

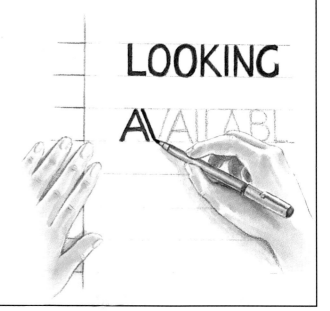

7 Using your thin black marker and a smaller letter size, write the other information below your heading and subheading, following the lines on the lined paper as needed. Leave lots of space around your name and phone number.

service

LOOKING FOR A SIT

AVAILABLE EVENING

I am 12 years old, a qu
baby-sitter, and I love kid

8 Photocopy as many flyers as you need. Use coloured pencils or markers to decorate or colour the flyers individually.

BABY-SITTING
service

LOOKING FOR A SITTER?
AVAILABLE EVENINGS

I am 12 years old, a qualified baby-sitter, and I love kids.
References available.

Call Mike
555-2595

GOOD IDEA: FUN WITH COLOURED PENCILS

If you press down heavily with a pencil, it makes a hard, firm line. If you draw lightly, the line is thinner and softer. You can use this technique to make some really fun effects with coloured pencils. Press down with a coloured pencil as you make the top part of a letter and soften your pressure as you come to the bottom. Try writing or printing a whole word this way. Then reverse the process — start with a light pressure and end with a heavy one. Try different colour combinations of paper and pencil. See what other patterns you can make by altering the pressure.

fading
away

dripping

coming

and

going

Calligram calendar

A calligram uses letters and words to make a picture. This project uses calligrams to illustrate the months of the year.

YOU WILL NEED

sheets of white paper 21.5 cm x 28 cm (8½ inches x 11 inches)

coloured pencils or thin markers

thin black marker

access to a photocopier

calendar for the year you want to make

four full-size pieces of coloured bristol board, cut into quarters 28 cm x 35.5 cm (11 inches x 14 inches)

hole punch

two hinged binder rings, 4 cm (1½ inches) in diameter

pencil, eraser, ruler, scissors, glue stick, scrap paper

1 On a scrap piece of paper, write down every month of the year. Beside each one, write as many words as you can think of to describe that month, or to describe things that happen during that month. For example:

January — cold, snow, frosty, blustery, bright

April — rain, soft, green, puddles, buds, wind, surprise, robin

July — sticky, hazy, thunderstorm, sunburn, cicada, sweaty

October — orange, yellow, red, apples, clear, frosty, sunny

2 Think of a simple picture you could draw to represent each month. A snowflake might be good for January, a robin for April, an ice-cream cone for July and a maple leaf for October.

3 Using a fresh piece of paper for each month, draw your pictures lightly in pencil.

4 Use coloured pencils or markers to write your descriptive words over the pencil lines. Vary the size of your letters, repeating or reversing words and using different colours. When you've finished, gently erase the pencil lines and cut out the shape. Now you have your calligram pages.

5 With a pencil, draw lines on a fresh piece of paper as follows:

6 Print the days of the week, beginning with Sunday, in the top row of boxes. Photocopy this page 14 times.

	3.5 cm (1⅜ in.)						
3.5 cm 1⅛ in.	Sunday	Monday	Tuesday	Wednesday	Thursday	Friday	Saturday
2.5 cm (1 in.) ← 3.0 cm (1¼ in.) →							

Down the page:
If you're using metric measurements, draw a line 3.5 cm from the left side of the page. If you're using imperial measurements, draw a line 1⅛ inches from the left side. From there, draw seven lines down the page, each one 3 cm (1¼ inches) apart, as shown.

Across the page:
Draw a line 3.5 cm (1⅜ inches) from the top of the page. From there, draw six lines across the page, each 2.5 cm (1 inch) apart.

Go over the lines with the black marker, as shown. Erase any pencil lines.

7 Using the Gothic lettering from page 12, print a month name at the top of each piece of paper. (You have two extras in case you make mistakes.) Use a calendar to write the dates on the correct day in each month. Mark down any holidays or birthdays. Now your month pages are ready.

8 Glue your January calligram onto a piece of bristol board and your January month page onto another. Glue your February calligram onto the back of your January month page, but place it upside-down compared to the month page. Glue your February month page onto another piece of bristol board, and your March calligram upside-down compared to it on the back. Repeat for all the months. You'll have three pieces of bristol board left over, and the months January and December will each have one blank side.

9 With your month pages facing you, make a mark 1.5 cm (½ inch) from the bottom in the centre of each bristol board. Make two additional marks 1.5 cm (½ inch) from the top and 4 cm (1½ inches) from the sides on each board. Use the hole punch to make holes in these three marks.

10 Stack your month and calligram pages in order. The holes should line up with each other. Put the hinged rings through the holes at the top of the months. Use the other hole to hang your calendar.

CHAPTER SIX

Beautiful letters

Unusual labels and tags can make something ordinary look extraordinary. These projects will show you how to use beautiful letters called Versals to make special gift tags and labels.

YOU WILL NEED

markers or coloured pencils

pencil, eraser, scrap paper

VERSAL LETTERS

Versal letters got their name because they were large initial letters that began verses in Bibles. They look very fancy, but they're easy to make once you get the hang of them. Versals are made of ovals with bulges and tree-trunk shapes.

1 On your scrap paper, draw an oval about 1 cm (³/₈ inch) high. Add bulges on either side. Colour the bulges in. You've made an O.

oval   bulges   completed

2 Make a tree trunk with an oval on its right side. Add a bulge to the oval. Put on a top and a bottom. Colour it in. It's a D.

tree   oval   bulge

top, bottom   completed

3 To make an A, start with a tree trunk. Add three-quarters of an oval on its left side. Make a curve coming out of the oval. Add a bulge, a top and a bottom. Draw a horizontal tree trunk and colour it in.

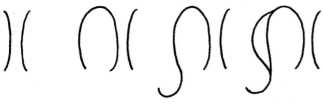 

| tree | oval | curve | bulge | top, bottom, horizontal tree | completed |

4 M is a round letter made of two ovals side by side. They form a tree trunk in the middle. Add bulges. Close off the top of the tree trunk. Draw a baseline for the whole thing to rest on. Colour it in.

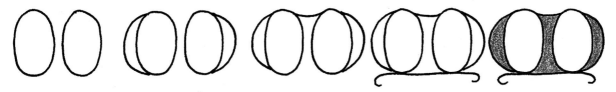

two ovals | bulges | close off top | baseline | completed

5 The letters you've just made will let you write MOM and DAD. Here's a complete Versal alphabet. See if you can find the ovals and tree trunks that make up the letters.

Gift tag

Next time you wrap a present, make it really special by writing the name on the tag in Versal letters.

YOU WILL NEED

a piece of white paper 12 cm x 21.5 cm (4¾ inches x 8½ inches)

thin black marker

markers or coloured pencils

gold marker (optional)

hole punch

a piece of ribbon, 0.5 cm x 25 cm (¼ inch x 10 inches)

pencil, eraser, ruler, scissors

1 Fold your paper in half lengthwise. Draw two guidelines 2.5 cm (1 inch) and 4 cm (1½ inches) from the bottom edge.

2 Use a pencil to write the name you want on your gift tag in Versal letters (page 36). Begin about 2 cm (¾ inch) from the left side of the paper and allow lots of room for each letter. These letters are wide — they can touch, but don't cram them together.

3 Finish the name. Go over the pencil lines with your thin black marker. Erase all guidelines and pencil lines. Then colour in the bulges with coloured pencils, markers, or, if you have it, a gold marker.

4 Trim the right-hand side of the paper, leaving about 2 cm (³/₄ inch) of space at the end of the name. Write your name and any message on the inside of the tag.

5 Punch a hole in the upper left corner of the tag and thread the ribbon through the hole. Tie the tag onto your gift.

Use Versal letters to make beautiful labels for gifts, school projects or collections. Write out your word or words on paper you like (note: coloured construction paper fades very quickly) and cut around your letters to form your label. Use a glue stick to attach it where you want.

CHAPTER SEVEN

Book works

In lettering, "illumination" usually means letters or decorations that are made of real gold. But you can make elegant book decorations without real gold. In this section you combine lettering you've already learned with vine ornamentation to make your own kind of beautiful illuminations.

YOU WILL NEED

an index card or a piece of heavy paper 12.5 cm x 20 cm (5 inches x 8 inches)

two thin markers, one black, one green

markers and coloured pencils

gold marker (optional)

hole punch

a piece of ribbon or yarn 25 cm (10 inches) long

pencil, eraser, ruler, scissors

BOOK MARK

Make this marker as a gift for your favourite book worm.

1 Cut your card or paper to measure 5 cm x 20 cm (2 inches x 8 inches).

2 Decide on a name to write on your book mark. Rule margin lines down the sides of the book mark about 1.5 cm ($^1/_2$ inch) from the edges.

3 Punch a hole about 1 cm ($^3/_8$ inch) from the top edge.

4 Beginning about 3 cm (1$^1/_4$ inches) from the top, write Versal letters (see page 36) down the middle of the book mark. If the name you are writing is very long, you'll have to make the letters smaller.

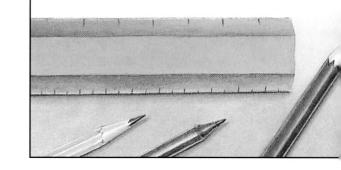

5 Draw a vine growing out of the left side of your first letter. If there is a curl or baseline, you can start there. Or pick a spot in the middle of the letter. Make the first strand of the vine "grow" down and along the left side of your book mark.

6 Add smaller branches by drawing vines that curl in the opposite direction from the original vine. Add smaller and smaller branches until you've filled as much of the space as you want. Don't let your curls get too tight, though — there's still more to add to these vines.

7 Add little twigs curling off the vines. These twigs are for leaves. Stagger them along both sides of the vines.

8 Draw simple leaf shapes at the end of the twigs. Add flowers or grapes at the ends of your vine branches. Fill the vine as much or as little as you like.

9 When you've completed your decoration, trace over the letters with your black marker. Trace over the vine with your green marker, then trace over the outlines of the leaves, flowers and grapes with the black marker.

10 Erase your pencil lines. Colour in your letters, leaves, flowers and grapes. If you have a gold marker, use it to fill in your letters for a truly illuminated effect.

11 Thread your ribbon or yarn through the hole. Tie it in a knot to attach it to the book mark.

Book plate

A book plate is a card or label that's added to the front of books to show who owns them.

1 On your paper, draw a rectangular box 10 cm x 8 cm (4 inches x 3⅛ inches). Rule guidelines on it from the top edge of the box as follows: at 1.5 cm, 2 cm, 2.5 cm, 3 cm, 4 cm, 4.5 cm, 5 cm, 6 cm, 6.5 cm, 7 cm (½ inch, ¾ inch, 1 inch, 1¼ inches, 1½ inches, 1¾ inches, 2 inches, 2¼ inches, 2½ inches, 2¾ inches).

2 Beginning about 2 cm (¾ inch) from the left side, print THIS BOOK in the first set of guidelines and BELONGS TO in the second set. Write in pencil first to see how your letters fit. Go over them in black marker.

3 Make a Versal letter (see page 36) for the first letter of your name between the guidelines at 4 cm (1½ inches) and 5 cm (2 inches). The length of your name will determine how close to the left edge you begin. Write the letter in pencil.

4 Pencil in the rest of your first name using the guidelines at 4.5 cm (1¾ inches) and 5 cm (2 inches) for your x-height. If you have a small-size calligraphy pen, you can do these letters in Gothic lettering (see page 12). You may have to change your guidelines a bit, depending on the size of your pen. See page 15 for changing pen sizes.

5 Repeat steps 3 and 4 in the next set of guidelines, writing your last name.

6 Draw a vine decoration in pencil off the first letter of your name as suggested on page 41. Fill the area all around your name. Keep the curves and curls round and open. Draw in the leaves, flowers and grapes wherever you like.

7 Go over your lines of decoration and your letters with black marker. Also go over the outline of your box. Erase all pencil marks and guidelines.

8 Photocopy as many book plates as you need, then cut them out. You can leave them black and white or you can colour them individually. Each one can be different.

9 Use a glue stick to glue your book plates into the front of your books.

VARIATION: ILLUMINATED STORY OR POEM

You can use Versal letters and vine illuminations the next time you write out a story or poem. Use the first letter of your text as a starting point for your decoration and decorate the margins as much as you like.

3-D letters

Letters are lines on a page. But they are also lines that enclose or make shapes. Those shapes can spring to life as sculptures.

YOU WILL NEED

a piece of light cardboard or bristol board 28 cm x 21.5 cm (11 inches x 8 1/2 inches)

cutting board

pencil, ruler, X-acto knife, glue stick

CONGRATULATIONS LETTER TOWER

Here's an unusual, 3-D congratulations card.

1 Make a line 2.5 cm (1 inch) from the edge of the short side of your cardboard. Press heavily with your pencil so you make an indentation. Divide the rest of the length of cardboard into four even vertical sections, each 6.5 cm (2 1/2 inches) wide. Press heavily when you make these lines.

2 Divide the board into four horizontal sections, each about 5.5 cm (2 1/8 inches) high. Don't worry if one is slightly shorter.

3 Beginning in the top left box, draw the letter C. Make it large enough for its edges to touch the sides of the box as shown. The stroke of the letter should be about 1 cm (³⁄₈ inch) wide all the way around. In the box below, draw the letter O in the same way. N goes next, then G in the bottom box of that row. Begin the next row with the letter R. Make sure each letter touches its neighbour along the top, sides and bottom. Keep going until you've finished the word CONGRATULATIONS. You'll have one box left at the bottom right. Leave that blank for now.

4 Use an X-acto knife to cut out carefully just the inside shapes of the letters — ask an adult to help you. Don't cut across the join lines.

5 Paint or decorate your letters. Use the uncut box as a place to write your name and message.

6 Fold along each vertical line. Trim the 2.5-cm (1-inch) strip to 1 cm (³⁄₈ inch). Fold it and glue it to the inside of the fourth edge to make a four-sided tower. Leave the tower on its side with a weight (such as your ruler) on the glued edge until it is dry.

GOOD IDEA: OTHER TOWERS

In the project design, you have room for 16 letters. If you need room for more, you can work out other designs on larger pieces of board or make the boxes smaller. For instance, you could use the cardboard lengthwise and make thinner letters. You could make a three-sided tower — this would work well to say "Get Well Soon." You could also divide the cardboard differently to make irregular-size letters. This would work well for "Happy Birthday."

Earrings

Dangle your initials from your ears with these beautiful, bright letter shapes.

YOU WILL NEED

acrylic modelling clay
such as Fimo

foil-lined cookie sheet

two 0.5-cm (¼-inch) jewellery rings

two fish-hook earring holders

pliers

1 Warm the clay in your hands. As it becomes soft, squeeze and knead it. Then roll it into a thin rope, about the width of a piece of spaghetti.

2 Make the initials in your name using the alphabet as shown. Each letter is made with only one rope of clay — the loops are made by twisting the clay over on itself. Each letter has a loop at the top for attaching a jewellery ring.

3 Carefully place your finished letters on the cookie sheet and bake them according to the instructions on the clay package.

4 When the letters are baked and cool, take them off the cookie sheet.

5 Bend a jewellery ring open with your pliers. Slip it onto a loop at the top of one of your initials. Hook the earring holder onto the open jewellery ring, making sure your letter will face forward when you wear it. Close the jewellery ring with the pliers. Repeat for your other initial.

6 If you have more than two initials in your name, you can hang a couple of letters on the same holder. You'll need to use a ring for each letter and attach the rings to the earring holders. The lines the letters make together will create wonderful and unexpected patterns.

VARIATION: PINS AND NECKLACES
Use your clay to make monogram pins and necklaces. Try combining initials on a backing in interesting arrangements. You can overlap letters or make several letters from one long rope.

KEEP LETTERING

7-98

Use the suggestions and ideas in this book to create lettering projects of your own. Look at books, ads, magazines and posters to see how letters are used. You'll find that letters come in thousands of shapes and sizes. Be a letter collector — if you see lettering you like, trace or copy it and keep it to use later. Experiment with different sizes, styles, tools and papers to invent new kinds of lettering. Most of all, enjoy the power in your fingers — the power to communicate your ideas on paper.